THE CARING AND INFINITE LOVE OF GOD

By
Dr. Beatriz Schiava
St. Louis, Missouri
2016

ANCIENT CHRISTIANITY PRESS

Título: THE CARING & INFINITE LOVE OF GOD
Autor: Dr. Beatriz Schiava M.D., M.T.S., M.A.
Book published by Ancient Christianity Press
A Division of Ancient Christianity & Amittai Press. L.L.C.
St. Louis, MO. U.S.A. www.ancientchristianitypress.com
Copyright 2016©Beatriz Schiava. All rights reserved.
Cover: "Let the little children come unto Me," by Carl Heinrich Bloch.

Bible references are taken from the New Revised Standard Version Bible,
copyright © 1989 the Division of Christian Education of the National
Council of the Churches of Christ in the United States of America. Used
by permission. All rights reserved; and Holy Bible, New Living
Translation, copyright © 1996, 2004, 2015 by Tyndale House Foundation.
Used by permission of Tyndale House Publishers Inc., Carol Stream,
Illinois 60188. All rights reserved. The Amplified® Bible (AMPC),
Copyright © 1954, 1958, 1962, 1964, 1965, 1987 by The Lockman
Foundation. Used by permission. www.Lockman.org;" Bible verses in
italics for emphasis.
Library of Congress Control Number: 2016942290

Love of God—Christianity. Theology—Religion. Spirituality—Jesus
Christ. Bible—Jesus Christ. Christianity—Gospel—Meditation.

ISBN: -978-0-9965673-1-2
ISBN:-10: 0-9965673-1-3
E-Book ISBN: 978-0-9965673-2-9
E-Book ISBN: 0-9965673-2-1
First edition: September 7, 2016. St. Louis, MO. U.S.
Printed in the United States of America.
10 9 8 7 6 5 4 3

GENERAL INDEX

And the grace of our Lord overflowed for me with the
faith and love that are in Christ Jesus.
—1 Timothy 1:14—

INTRODUCTION

We *love because He first loved us*, (1 John 4:19).[1] When the Lord with great compassion and tenderness touched us with His Grace and saved us, we began a journey with Him full of blessings. His love reaches every human who is open to receive it and delivers the mighty power of God, transforming our lives, and the lives of those whom His providence draws near to us.

This book is about the love of God. It is about His amazing love that gives us the strength and the courage to live every day with joy in our hearts; God's marvelous love transforms us into His likeness and gives us the inspiration we need to serve others and to love our neighbor as ourselves. In this book we also talk about God's compassionate love, that fills us with the hope we cling to, the comfort and His peace that surpasses all understanding,[2] during the toughest difficulties of life and our deepest sufferings; God's amazing love gives purpose and direction to our lives, and helps us to live a life of contentment and fulfillment; His tender love inspires us to live separate from sin; God's love is the best deterrent to sin, avoiding all the unnecessary suffering and pain caused by the consequences of sin.

The goal of this book is to help you, dear reader, to reflect on the love of God, and to understand more completely, *how wide and long and high and deep is the love of Christ*, (Ephesians 3:18). We first begin to experience the caring, tender, and the infinite

1

love of God with the realization of how much He loves us; it is His love that saves us. Our hearts are overjoyed when we exclaim: God's Grace touched me! His Grace reached for me! I will never be alone! I will never be the same!

Jesus is always with us; the darkness that was like a mist preventing us from seeing the right path, has been replaced by His amazing light, ever brighter, that shines in our darkness, illuminating our whole beings. Our hearts, through His grace, open to the reality that Jesus was thinking in each one of us when He willingly went to the Cross carrying our sins to free us from the slavery of sin. We were completely washed in His blood, and He forgave of all our sins, to live truly free of the guilt of sin. However, salvation and forgiveness of sins mark the beginning of our journey with the Lord. God loves us so much that cannot leave us broken as we were when we first came to Him.

Jesus' love is unconditional, and He desires our happiness. However, He cannot do anything without our free choice to accept His help. He desires to heal our souls so we can reach our full potential as human beings and to discover that our purpose in life is to love our neighbor and to serve Him through serving others. He wants that we discover in Him our reason to live, by making Him the center of our lives because He is our true happiness. Jesus is waiting for us with open arms to say:

Yes, Jesus! Please transform me into your likeness!
Please, make me new!

Yes, Jesus, heal my soul, my body, and the suffering that still clutches my heart!

Yes, Jesus, give me your Holy Spirit, and teach me how to live for you and for all those who I come in contact with!

Yes, Jesus, please, make me whole, and give me a loving, compassionate, and caring heart!

And Jesus, please, never, ever, let me go from your presence!

I know you heard this humble prayer! Thank you, Jesus!

In the Name of the Father, through Your Precious Name, Jesus, my Savior, Amen!

By our own free will and cooperation with Him, Jesus Christ transforms us into His likeness little by little, tenderly and gently, throughout our lives. Jesus will close our wounds, taking the debris and dirt out, healing them with His love. On top of this, He will give us a new heart, full of love, kindness, and compassion for others. His love will fill our hearts and we will go on living with Him, eternally. Once we have decided to follow our dear Savior, Jesus, His love, and His hope, will not abandon us because *We are His Masterpiece, He has created us anew in Christ Jesus, so we can do the good things he planned for us long ago,* (Ephesians 2:10).

The journey in fellowship with Jesus started when we were born again, and we entrusted our lives to Him, but does not end there. We will walk with Him during this life, until the joyous day, when we see each other face to face in His Heavenly Kingdom. In this book, we review what the word of God says about the love of God. While His love is beyond our

3

comprehension, we can experience His love if we are open to receive it.

As we experience the love of God through His Holy Spirit, we experience peace and contentment. We realize that His love is our true happiness! If we have Jesus, we have it all: *The LORD is my shepherd; I have all that I need*, (Psalm 23:1). When we choose to follow His instructions, precepts, and commandments with the help of His Holy Spirit, we find true peace and contentment that does not depend on our material possessions, prestige, or a life without difficulties, but on our relationship with Jesus.

A close relationship with God depends on our knowledge of Him, on obedience to His Word, and on trusting Him, by complete surrender of our whole beings to Jesus Christ. Our relationship with God through His Son Jesus Christ should be one of trust, knowing that the *Lord is good. His unfailing love continues forever, and his faithfulness continues to each generation*, (Ps. 100:5). Through every event of our lives, He is with us, because God's love for us does not depend on our feelings or our emotions, but His love is constant, faithful, unconditional, powerful, always at hand, and everlasting. Dear reader, you can experience His love by knowing Him better through His Word.

In this book you will find, dear reader, a great selection of Bible verses that have inspired Christians to love Him with every inch of their hearts, for the past 2000 years. This book is also a plea for us to return to the heart of Jesus, to know Him better and accept his caring and infinite love.

I want to share with you, dear reader, this loving and caring God, the Holy One, and His Son Jesus Christ. His light, ever brighter, enlightens my darkness and soften the difficulties of life. I rejoice in His Salvation! It is such a treasure, a once in a lifetime gift, that was paid in full by Jesus on the cross! Nothing else is needed, yet, with His Salvation, this generous and loving God adds so many blessings! Jesus said: *Seek the Kingdom of God above all else, and live righteously, and he will give you everything you need,* (Matthew 6:33).[3]

We are always in debt with the Lord; there is nothing we can do to repay His generosity. The apostle Paul reminds us: "God saved you by his grace when you believed. And you can't take credit for this; it is a gift from God. Salvation is not a reward for the good things we have done, so none of us can boast about it," (Ephesians 2:8-9).

My prayer, dear reader, is that this book blesses you richly. May His love and blessings overflow in your heart, and you discover and experience His Infinite and Caring Love for you:

"But thanks be to God, who in Christ always leads us in triumph, and through us, spreads the fragrance of the knowledge of him everywhere," (2 Corinthians 2:14).

Beatriz Schiava, MD, MTS, MA.
St. Louis, Missouri.
United States of America.
September 7, 2016.

CHAPTER 1

THE LOVE OF GOD

"For God so loved the world that he gave his only Son, so
that everyone who believes in Him may not perish but may
have eternal life."
—John 3:16—

L ove comes from God because *God is love,* (1 John 4:7-8).
We are a reflection of the love of God because He is the
source of love. It is natural for us to feel and experience
love. Since we were babies, we knew the warm sensation of
love in our hearts. We experience love for our dear ones, for our
pets, and for nature. We feel love when we see our loved ones
and we feel their love for us. We feel happy and want to share
with those we love, our time and our mutual experiences.

We care about our loved ones and what happens in their
lives; thus, we are eager to be acquainted with even the most
nominal details of their lives. We give gifts to the ones we love,
not expecting anything in return, but because we want to make
them happy. We experience feelings of love and tenderness for
our children. We care for them by providing for their needs, by
complimenting them, and by helping them to see their mistakes
and learn from them. We love our children by teaching them to
love and honor God, to be law-abiding members of society, and
future responsible, loving spouses and parents.

Our beloved pets also become part of our lives and important family members, whom we love and care for. We care for our friends, and our neighbors, and even for those who we don't know, but are in need. Many sacrifice their lives for a loved one, and some even for a stranger. We see on TV, stories of altruism that inspire and amaze us. A man who risks his life to rescue children out of a burning home; a complete stranger donates his kidney to a person he doesn't even know. These are just a few examples of incredible acts of altruism and love of neighbor. Yet, even while we have a great capacity to love, our human love can never be compared with the caring, perfect, infinite, and unconditional love of God.

When we get to know God and comprehend how much God loves us and cares for us, we find an unending source of love, confidence, purpose, happiness and joy that can completely inspire and transform our lives, and give true meaning to our existence. Nobody will ever love us like God loves us. His love is unconditional and perfect, greater than any feeling of love we have ever experienced:

"For as the heavens are high above the earth, so great is his steadfast love toward those who fear him," (Psalm 103:11).

Jesus Christ, the Son of God is the greatest proof that God loves us. It is inconceivable, mind blowing, that any one of us would give away his only son, knowing that in the near future he would be crucified. Yet, God the Father did exactly that; this is the depth of His love for humanity! It is also unimaginable, truly unthinkable, that the Son said yes to his Father, laying down His life to save humanity. Jesus knew beforehand, the kind of emotional and physical suffering he would have to endure, and the inconceivable death he would suffer, and yet, He was willing:

"The Father loves me, because I am willing to give up my life, in order that I may receive it back again. No one takes my life away from me. I give it up of my own free will. I have the right to give it up, and I have the right to take it back. This is what my Father has commanded me to do," (John 10:17-18).[4]

Jesus Christ, the Son of God, knew that many of the people he intended to save did not want to be saved. As it was during His apprehension, trial, and crucifixion, many people in the future would betray Him, insult Him, mock Him, despise Him, and reject Him all over again. Yet the Son of God willingly went to the cross for us, even for those who would reject Him. God the Father and His Son Jesus love us with infinite, immeasurable love. Jesus said:

"And it is the will of him who sent me that I should not lose any of all those he has given me, but that I should raise them all to life on the last day. For what my Father wants is that all who see the Son and believe in him should have eternal life. And I will raise them to life on the last day,"(John 6:39-40).

CHAPTER 2

JESUS OUR TRUE HAPPINESS

He who gives heed to the word will prosper, and happy is
he who trusts in the LORD.
—Proverbs 16:20—

Jesus, the Son of God, who is God and One with God, for His immense love for humanity became a human being to be the light in our darkness, our hope, and true happiness: "In this the love of God was made manifest among us, that God sent his only Son into the world, so that we might live through him. In this is love, not that we loved God, but that he loved us and sent his Son to be the expiation for our sins," (1 John 4:9-10).

God the Father, through His Son Jesus Christ reaches for us because He does not want his children to be lost, but He desires that we come to Him, who is true love, and true life. Jesus suffered death on the cross, to reconcile us with the Father, to save humanity and give us eternal life:

"But God shows his love for us in that while we were yet sinners Christ died for us. Since, therefore, we are now justified by his blood, much more shall we be saved by him from the wrath of God. For if while we were enemies, we were reconciled to God by the death of his Son, much more, now that we are reconciled, shall we be saved by his life," (Rom 5:8-10).

9

The Lord went to extremes to reach for us. Jesus gave His life for us to reconcile us with God and to have friendship with Him:

"For if while we were enemies, we were reconciled to God through the death of his Son, much more surely, having been reconciled, will we be saved by his life. But more than that, we even boast in God through our Lord Jesus Christ, through whom we have now received reconciliation," (Romans 5:10-11).

When we give our life to Jesus Christ and submit to His will, we trust Him with our lives, and we know that He will take great care of us because we are His children. Regardless of the situation, we are confident that because of Jesus death on the cross and that *He was raised for our justification*, God hears our prayers. We know that Jesus lives and cares for us.[5] He will listen to our requests and give us His very best because He loves us. We also have His testament of love, the Bible, to learn His Will for our lives and how to live close to Him. God's word is our guidance, to live a life of abundance and blessings, and to avoid mistakes in life that cause us suffering: "The thief comes only to steal and kill and destroy; I came that they may have life, and have it abundantly," (John 10:10).

The thief is Satan and he is the *god of this world*.[6] Satan and his fallen angels offer money, lust, material things, drugs, greed and power, to distract us from our purpose, the perfect and sweet way of the Lord. Whoever loves the world and follows its deceitful path, will not stop until he gets his way, sometimes breaking the commandments of God, and our government's laws. All the ways of Satan result in slavery to sin, death, destruction and suffering. If Satan gets his way with us, he will ultimately destroy us and separate us from God eternally.

Satan blinds people, convincing them to substitute money, luxury, pleasures of the flesh for God. This fallen angel, called Lucifer, twists the reality with lies and deceptions. He fills us with fear, to make us think there are no solutions to our problems that all hope is lost. Satan fills us with despair and whispers in our ears that we are alone in this world, that there is no escape or salvation.

Satan uses politically correct language; he uses nothing more than half-truths; if Satan told the truth, he would stop being Satan, the father of lies; but when he tells a bold lie, it is easily detected that he is lying to us. Satan's ancient method is to tell half-truths, lies disguised as truths, hiding useful information from us to take the best decisions. Satan conceals from us the disastrous consequences the counsel of the world brings to us.

This is why Satan's half-truths told without consequences are so appealing. Under such premises, decisions look right and very attractive, even as they are immoral and harmful. In the end, they will cause great suffering and destruction to us, and to others.

For example, a woman can abort a baby thinking that the baby will change her life for the worse. The world arguments are: The laws of this world approve abortions; the baby is not really a human being; the rights of a woman are first, and to give preference to her way of living over the life of the baby is right and acceptable. We frequently hear, "it is my body, I can do whatever I want with it." These are the lies many have come to believe.

When the truth is told, that it is a baby, not a product, but a human being, who can feel pain as early as 8 weeks, such realization is offensive to many and causes anger and rejection.[7] Yet, the origin of the word *fetus* is from the Latin, [8] and means "offspring." Our way of life becomes idolatry when it is our own pleasure, and nothing and nobody else matters.

The world says: "live free, and do as you want, follow your heart, or do as your heart compels you." Yet, by disregarding the consequences, many have caused great damage to others and destruction. Even if the world approves abortion, late term abortion, or infanticide, we Christians know that we have to respect life. It is especially heinous to inflict pain and murder the defenseless, the smallest among us. Even when it is against popular consensus, we have to protect those who cannot make their voice heard; we have to show love of neighbor to the unborn and their mothers. It is Christian love of neighbor to protect the unborn because their lives belong to God. We know the baby is not at fault, but he or she is a great gift of God, who must be honored as such, in the sanctity of the womb. It is not a product, but a baby who feels and suffers, and experiences love, a reflection of the love our Maker and compassionate God has for all His children:

"You made all the delicate, inner parts of my body and knit me together in my mother's womb. Thank You for making me so wonderfully complex! Your workmanship is marvelous—how well I

12

know it. You watched me as I was being formed in utter seclusion, as I was woven together in the dark of the womb. You saw me before I was born. Every day of my life was recorded in Your book. Every moment was laid out before a single day had passed," (Psalm 139: 13-16).[9]

God wants to set us on the path of righteousness because he does not want us to suffer, but to be happy and have a life with abundant blessings. If we do the things the Lord has instructed us to do, love our neighbor as ourselves, the consequences will be good. Most of the time, we will not suffer, but even if we suffer for doing the right thing, the Lord will reward us: *it is better to suffer for doing good, if that is what God wants, than to suffer for doing wrong!*

To obey our hearts by ignoring the wisdom of the Word of God, His commandments and instructions, can bring us great suffering: *the human heart is the most deceitful of all things, and desperately wicked. Who really knows how bad it is?* (Jeremiah 17:9). The wisdom of God, in His Word, wants us to be free from the slavery of sin, and therefore, to be free from the self-inflicted suffering that is the end result of our sins.

How can we, imperfect beings, trust our human hearts, if we are constantly changing our minds as part of growing, unaware of our lack of knowledge regarding the challenges we face day by day? The law, the commandments, instructions, and the heart of God do not change, even as the world changes around us. We are all fallible, and in the past, when we were ignorant of the word of God, we made serious mistakes, that caused us immense suffering and sorrow. Regardless of the many errors we have incurred in the past, the Lord forgives us if we ask Him: *But if we confess our sins to him, he is faithful and just to forgive us our sins and to cleanse us from all wickedness,* (1 John 1:9). The Lord washes us in His blood and gives us a clean slate to start again without guilt. God gives us his Holy Spirit to live separated from sin, following in the footsteps of Jesus: *Therefore, if any person is [ingrafted] in Christ (the Messiah) he is a new creation (a new creature altogether); the old [previous moral and spiritual condition] has passed away. Behold, the fresh and new has come!* (2 Corinthians 5:17).[10]

The only way we can follow the Lord, and love Him is by knowing Him. By the same token, the best motivation to live separate from sin, and not to reap unnecessary suffering as a consequence of sin, is to experience the unconditional love of God:

"This is what the LORD says: "Don't let the wise boast in their wisdom, or the powerful boast in their power, or the rich boast in their riches. But those who wish to boast should boast in this alone: that they truly know Me and understand that I am the LORD, who demonstrates unfailing love and who brings justice and righteousness to the earth, and that I delight in these things. I, the LORD, have spoken!" (Jeremiah 9:23-24).[11]

Sometimes we experience difficult situations in life; we are not guilty of wrongdoing, yet we suffer the consequences of the sins of those close to us. Moreover, we suffer disease, natural disasters, economic downturns, political and social turmoil that affect our lives, and we see our loved ones suffer through illnesses or death. When a person learns to love God and

14

depends on Him, despite the difficulties he may encounter in life, he finds peace in the midst of adversity, and in his weakness, he relies on the strength of the Lord; he will trust in Him, and because of his faith, he will live with hope, regardless of the hardship and sorrow; he knows, he is certain, Jesus loves him and remains with him through it all! This Christian knows that all circumstances are temporal, but the plans of the Lord will prevail. He is full of blessings, peace, contentment and hope because he knows about the Lord promises and does what pleases the Lord; he knows he has a present full of the presence of God and an eternal future with Him in His Heavenly Kingdom:

"For I know the plans I have for you," says the LORD. "They are plans for good and not for disaster, to give you a future and a hope," (Jeremiah 29:11).

The Word of God helps us to know God and His Son Jesus Christ. When we are alone reading about His promises, about His beautiful plans for us, about Jesus' life full of the love of neighbor, service, and selfless sacrifice, we learn to love Him, and appreciate each time a little more the fathomless, unending love that God has for us. If we really want to follow God and experience His infinite love, we have to make the decision to commit to follow Jesus or to reject Him: "He who is not with Me [*definitely on My side*] is against Me, and he who does not [*definitely*] gather with Me and for My side scatters," (Matthew 12:30).[12]

The first psalm in the Bible introduces the reader to the two ways every human being chooses from: to accept God's love and friendship, or to reject Him, and the consequences that this decision entails. The first three verses of the first psalm explain who the friend of God is, and the blessings, joy, and prosperity the believer obtains. The last three verses explain who the enemy of God is and what his end is:

"BLESSED (HAPPY, fortunate, prosperous, and enviable) is the man who walks and lives, not in the counsel of the ungodly [*following their advice, their plans and purposes*], nor stands [*submissive and inactive*] in the path where sinners walk, nor sits down [*to relax and rest*] where the scornful [*and the mockers*] gather. But his delight and desire are in the law of the Lord, and on His law (the precepts, the instructions, the teachings of God) he habitually meditates (ponders and studies) by day and by night. And he shall be like a tree firmly planted [*and tended*] by the streams of water, ready to bring forth its fruit in its season; its leaf also shall not fade or wither; and everything he does shall prosper [*and come to maturity*]."

"Not so the wicked [*those disobedient and living without God are not so*]. But they are like the chaff [*worthless, dead, without substance*] which the wind drives away. Therefore, the wicked [*those disobedient and living without God*] shall not stand [*justified*] in the judgment, nor sinners in the congregation of the righteous [*those who are upright and in right standing with God*]. For the Lord knows and is fully acquainted with the way of the righteous, but the way of the ungodly [*those living outside God's will*] shall perish, (end in ruin and come to nought)," (Psalm 1:1-6).[13]

Similarly, Jesus taught the two ways: You can enter God's Kingdom only through the narrow gate. The highway to hell is broad, and its gate is wide for the many that choose that way.

(Mt 7:13). The narrow gate, the gate of life,[14] is the door of those who choose to do the Will of God and gave their lives to Jesus. They crucified the flesh, living separated from sin to walk in the Spirit. Jesus said, But the gateway to life is very narrow and the road is difficult, and only a few ever find it, (Matthew 7:14).

We need to drench ourselves in the Word of God, to know the will of God for our lives and to find the treasures and blessings of His Kingdom. We learn from the Word of God, His precious wisdom, to discern between the truth, the right path of life, and the false path that leads to destruction.

The Word of God uncovers the deception in our lives and in the world. We are used to, and even ignore, wrongful patterns of behavior, false beliefs, and misconceptions that hurt those around us and cause us suffering. The Word of God teaches us the truth so we can rectify our lives, and help us through His Holy Spirit to be more like Jesus.

The Word of God must fall constantly in the heart, like living waters flowing on a rough and acute edged rock, to give it shape, polishing it, until the rock no longer has edges and cannot hurt to the touch. By the constant rubbing of His living waters, our hearts are not anymore made of stone, but He gives us instead, a heart of flesh with a smooth, lovely surface, refined, porous to the inflow and outflow of His living waters. Those *rivers of living water*[15] penetrate even the smallest spaces of the heart, and the Word becomes the guide and the very substance by which we live our lives. Jesus' love takes away the impurities and through His sacrifice makes us worthy to inherit the Kingdom of God. He makes our heart even more beautiful and precious than the magnificent sapphires and emeralds of His Kingdom, purer and clearer than the *sea of glass sparkling like a crystal* [16] in front of the Throne of God:

A new heart I will give you, and a new spirit I will put within you; and I will remove from your body the heart of stone and give you a heart of flesh, (Ezekiel 36:26).

Come to the living waters of His love; let Him give shape to your heart. Let Him polish you and *delight in you with gladness,*[17] while your heart lies in His loving hands. Submit to His tender, gentle love and care, until you are completely immersed in His love, becoming as He is, true love of a kind and compassionate heart. Everything pales when compared to the knowledge of God, which is the greatest treasure anyone can possess. It is so great and so rich that not even a lifetime suffices to extract every jewel, every gorgeous pearl of Wisdom.

The tool we are given to excavate this magnificent treasure is meditation. The word "meditation,"[18] in the Bible is to ponder, to study, to murmur continuously His precious Word, to reflect thoughtfully upon the Word of God, and our behavior in the light of His Word. Meditation enables us to save his precepts, instructions and commands not only in the mind, but also deep in the heart.

When meditation is effective, the wisdom of God becomes embedded in the heart, creating positive changes in the life of the believer. God empowers the believer with His grace, His love and His compassion, giving us a burning desire to love our neighbor with all our hearts. When we meditate on Jesus' life in the middle of our desert, thirsty for Him, Jesus Christ provides for us His living waters, and we thirst no more, rejoicing in our salvation.[19]

Meditate on Jesus' love for you, on His honesty, on His great compassion for those ill from body and soul, and you will find the very source of love you need to give you rest and peace in difficult situations, loving your neighbor as yourself. Meditate on Jesus Christ's defense for the defenseless, on His sacrificial love, giving His life for us on the Cross, and you will find His strength in your weakness and His joyful hope to go on, despite the sufferings of this life. Meditate on Jesus' unconditional love for you with tears of joy, on His absolute forgiveness and His mercy, and you will be able to forgive yourself; free from guilt, you will find the grace of God and in the remembrance of His sufferings, the strength to live separated from sin.

In the silence of your room, meditate on Jesus glorious and majestic resurrection; you will remember then, to focus on Jesus and on His heavenly Kingdom; for we are waiting for the soon return of our Lord, and the glorious day, we will be with Him, embraced by His love, resting in His bosom.

Dear reader, the goal should not be to read the Bible in one year, but the goal must be the constant meditation of the Word of God, meditating on the life of Jesus in the gospels, a little bit at a time, for as many years as we have of life, to let the Holy Spirit transform us into His likeness. Through the breathing of His Holy Spirit in us, prayer, meditation on the Word of God, and the practice of love of neighbor, our faith, that is a gift of God, increases. We become more aware of the presence of God and the authority of the Holy Spirit in our daily lives. We begin to trust more in the Lord as our relationship with God becomes closer. His love inspires us to make radical life changes to live separated from sin, clothed with the holiness of Jesus, and in friendship with God. We are born again! We are truly a new creation in Christ:

Since you have heard about Jesus and have learned the truth that comes from Him, throw off your old sinful nature and your former way of life, which is corrupted by lust and deception. Instead, let the Spirit renew your thoughts and attitudes. Put on your new nature, created to be like God — truly righteous and holy, (Ephesians 4:21-24).

God's love, when combined with our salvation is the greatest blessing one can possess. If you have in your heart His love, you will not compare yourself to anyone else, because His infinite love for you is all you need and all you will ever want. If you have the wonderful love of Jesus deep in your heart, you will love yourself, and will be patient with your mistakes instead of putting yourself down. He loved you first, just like you are, and more than you ever will love yourself: *We love because he first loved us,* (1 John 4:19). God has infinite patience with each one of us, simply because, He loves us and wants us to be happy: "The LORD is merciful and compassionate, slow to get angry and filled with unfailing love," (Psalm 145:8);[20] God is our true happiness: "With joy, you will draw water from the wells of salvation," (Isaiah 12:3).

True happiness is to know God, to love Him and to obey His Word; it is, indeed, the Kingdom of God in our midst:[21] *for the kingdom of God is not food and drink but righteousness and peace and joy in the Holy Spirit,* (Romans 14:17). Jesus is the Holy Face of God, the Father; if we love Jesus by knowing and obeying His Word, we also know the Father: *If you know me, you will know my Father also. From now on you do know him and have seen him,* (John 14:7). To know and love God is truly the greatest purpose in life! To know Him and be known by Him is truly the greatest treasure!

CHAPTER 3

THE LOVE OF GOD
IN THE MIDST OF TRIALS

"Dear brothers and sisters, when troubles come your way, consider it an opportunity for great joy. For you know that when your faith is tested, your endurance has a chance to grow. So let it grow, for when your endurance is fully developed, you will be perfect and complete, needing nothing."[22]
—James 1:2-4—

We come to the Lord as spiritual babies, who need nourishment and great patience. God takes care of each one of us as beloved children; we receive from Him, our daily bread, and our true manna that never perishes through His precious Word. While we stumble to walk, and many times slip and fall, He grabs our hands and helps us to stand up. As we mature in His ways, we are never far from the loving arms and the bosom of God. He tenderly cares for us and disciplines us to become future heirs of His Kingdom. The trials of this life strengthen our faith and our relationship with God; they help us to grow spiritually for our final destiny, to be citizens of heaven[23] and to live eternally in union with God the Father and His beloved Son Jesus, our Savior. Adversity in life, suffering, and even calamities are just the temporal tests we need to overcome. We overcome with the righteousness of God, and through prayer, asking for the strength of the Lord in our weaknesses, drawing us closer to Him. In each of these trials and sufferings, there is a glorious step taken, drawing us ever closer to the mansion that Jesus has prepared for us in His heavenly Kingdom.[24]

In his second letter to the Corinthians, Paul writes about his sufferings, his multiple times in prison, and his flagellation. Paul was stoned three times; beaten with rods, persecuted, suffered cold, hunger, and thirst. He was shipwrecked, in danger many times of dying, and he had the burden of keeping all the new Christian communities faithful to the Good News of our Lord Jesus Christ in the midst of persecutions.[25] Adding to all his sufferings, Paul had a physical illness that tormented him. Three times Paul asked the Lord to remove that immense suffering that he describes as, "a thorn in the flesh."[26]

Were all these sufferings allowed by God because He did not love Paul? No! On the contrary! Paul was a very blessed man whom the Lord favored and set apart for His service. Jesus saved him from eternal damnation since Paul had zealously persecuted Christians in the past, having them imprisoned and condemned to death.[27]

The apostle Paul, known formerly as Saul of Tarsus, studied to be a Pharisee, under the guidance of Gamaliel, a Pharisee, a doctor of the Law.[28] Saul was "thoroughly trained in the law of his ancestors."[29] He relentlessly persecuted Christians and was "zealous for God."[30] Saul, as many Pharisees did, considered Christians apostates, infidels and blasphemers.[31] Jesus had foreseen the persecution of the nascent Church and warned his disciples:

"They will put you out of the synagogues; indeed, the hour is coming when whoever kills you will think he is offering service to God. And they will do this because they have not known the Father, nor me, "(John 16:2-3).

Saul, a Pharisee, highly trained and educated, and yet, he forgot the commandment of the Lord: "You shall not murder;" "You shall not take vengeance or bear any grudge against the sons of your own people, but you shall love your neighbor as yourself: I am the LORD," (Exodus 20:13; Leviticus 19:18). Saul did not know true love and compassion because he did not know God. Hence, he was not able to love his neighbor, as himself: *He who does not love does not know God; for God is love*, (1 John 4:8). Saul knew religion, a set of traditions, rites, and even vestments to worship and please God, but did not have a personal, intimate relationship with God, whose fruit is the love of neighbor. In His religious fervor, in his zeal, Saul thought that he loved God, and was defending his faith, but instead, he was full of religious fanaticism and hate for those who worship God in a different way.

Saul's wrongful, irrational ideology, took him to threaten, imprison, and murder Jews and Gentiles, including women and children, who did not follow his religious convictions. Saul's religion was a way to earn the love of God, to earn his own salvation. Saul was burning with the desire to murder, for he believed it justified the purity of his religion. It was hate that fed his soul and his obsession, not the love of God. In his ideology, there was pride, spiritual blindness, hatred, ignorance of God, and madness. He worshiped God with a heart of stone and although he had eyes to see, he was truly blind spiritually.[32]

Sadly, in our times, there are many "Sauls," who believe that murder gets them closer to God. These Sauls believe that God will open the doors of heaven by the slaughtering of His children, in whom God lives eternally, and for whom God suffers, seeing them so cruelly persecuted!

Jesus Christ changed drastically Saul's life, by loving him unconditionally. Our Lord Jesus touched Saul with His grace, extending His love to Saul and saving him. He became a new man in Jesus Christ and he will forever be known as the apostle Paul. It is the love of God with the realization of his spiritual blindness that changed Saul.

Jesus loved Saul, even when he had a feverish obsession to murder Christians and was dominated by hate in his heart. The light of the Lord flashed around him on his way to Damascus, where he was to persecute even more Christians; "Paul fell to the ground, and heard a voice saying "'Saul! Saul! Why are you persecuting me?"' "Who are you, Lord?" Saul asked. And the voice replied, "I am Jesus, the one you are persecuting!"[33]

By persecuting Christians, Saul was persecuting Jesus. When we sin against another human being, we are sinning against God: *And the King will answer them, 'Truly, I say to you, as you did it to one of the least of these my brethren, you did it to me,'*(Matthew 25:40). The light of God blinded Saul's physical eyes, but now he was able to see spiritually. Saul fasted and prayed with a yearning heart and humbleness, and the Lord healed him. Ananias put his hands on him and the scales of his eyes fell and received the Holy Spirit.[34] Immediately, Saul got baptized, he was born again as Paul, with the right to be called apostle of Jesus. Then Paul ate, and *at once* he began to preach the Gospel, (Acts: 17-19). From all his letters, and the Acts of the Apostles, we can surmise that Paul once persecuted the Church with incredible zeal, but when he gave his life to Jesus, he used the same passion for embracing the Church and for preaching the Gospel. Paul spread the Gospel even in prison, knowing he was going to be put to death. In the end, Paul died by decapitation at the hands of the Roman Empire.[35]

Paul was prepared to die for the Church of Christ, to give his own blood, for Christ's Bride, for the children of God, *who are the living stones that God is building into his spiritual temple,*[36] imitating the sacrificial love of Jesus Christ. Paul wrote to the Philippians:

"But I will rejoice even if I lose my life, pouring it out like a liquid offering to God, just like your faithful service is an offering to God. And I want all of you to share that joy. Yes, you should rejoice, and I will share your joy," (Philippians 2:17-18).[37]

Paul, the man who persecuted with incredible hate the Church was in Christ, *a new creation,*[38] a new man ready and willing to give his life for Jesus and His Church. On the eve of his death Paul wrote: *As for me, my life has already been poured out as an offering to God. The time of my death is near,* (2 Timothy 4:6).[39]

Paul received from the Lord many visions; he saw paradise and received many revelations. However, such blessings did not come without great sacrifice and many afflictions. Thus, the

Lord did not remove the thorn in the flesh that tormented him: "And to keep me from being too elated by the abundance of revelations, a thorn was given me in the flesh, a messenger of Satan, to harass me, to keep me from being too elated. Three times I besought the Lord about this, that it should leave me; but he said to me, "My grace is sufficient for you, for my power is made perfect in weakness," (2 Corinthians 12: 7-9). Pride is the greatest enemy of our friendship with God. Whenever we have in our lives struggle, retaliation, fights, greed, lack of forgiveness, resentment, there is pride. God's Word advice to us is to *live at peace with everyone,*[40] to forgive, to love instead of hate,[41] and to overlook the offense.[42]

Jesus said: *Take my yoke upon you. Let me teach you, because I am humble and gentle at heart, and you will find rest for your souls,* (Matthew11:29);[43] *But when you are praying, first forgive anyone you are holding a grudge against, so that your Father in heaven will forgive your sins, too,* (Mark 11:25).[44]

Paul learned from Jesus obedience and humility; submitting entirely to the will of God requires humility and obedience. If in his past life, the Apostle Paul was proud of his education, of his accomplishments, and even of murdering Christians, in his new life in Jesus Christ, Paul boasted of the Christ crucified, who saved him by His amazing grace that touched his life and changed it forever; he boasted and rejoiced of his weaknesses because they allowed the power of God to rest in him. Talking about his new life in Christ, Paul wrote:

"May I never boast of anything except the cross of our Lord Jesus Christ, by which the world has been crucified to me, and I to the world," (Galatians 6:14).

God refused to take away the "thorn in the flesh" that Paul was suffering to keep him humble: "My grace is sufficient for you, for power is made perfect in weakness;"[45] Paul replied to God's answer:

"So, I will boast all the more gladly of my weaknesses, so that the power of Christ may dwell in me. Therefore, I am content with weaknesses, insults, hardships, persecutions, and calamities for the sake of Christ; for whenever I am weak, then I am strong." (2 Corinthians 12:9b-10).

God does not give us what we want, but He gives us, as the caring and loving father God is, what we really need. The apostle Paul needed a reminder in his flesh to keep him humble and submitted to the will of God. Pride could have destroyed his ministry. Paul understood the calling of the Lord was not only an undeserved privilege, but it was also, a source of great suffering. Jesus told to Ananias: "And I will show him how much he must suffer for my name's sake," (Acts 9:16).

Yet, Paul embraced the suffering because he held tightly to Jesus' love to remain joyful, optimistic, and even happy in the midst of suffering, physical afflictions, and even in the face of death. Paul had experienced the love of God and learned to love God in any situation in life. He loved Jesus Christ even more than he loved himself, and through His divine love and grace, he preached the Gospel with great humility and love for his fellow Christians.

Paul received the unconditional love of God, and this love was the engine that propelled him to preach the Gospel even in the most adverse situations. The apostle Paul was very aware that his salvation was granted not by his merits or his works, but it was the gift of God; thus, he was immensely grateful!

"I am grateful to Christ Jesus our Lord, who has strengthened me, because he judged me faithful and appointed me to his service, even though I was formerly a blasphemer, a persecutor, and a man of violence. But I received mercy because I had acted ignorantly in unbelief," (1 Timothy 1:12-13).

Paul obtained his salvation by God's Grace and by the merit of Jesus Christ on the cross. Jesus gave His life for him, [46] and for Paul, that was the ultimate proof of God's love for Him. Paul experienced so fully the love of God, that Paul became, through His Grace, into His likeness, to share the powerful and compassionate love of God. Thus, Paul imitated Jesus Christ, even in His sacrificial love, "pouring out" his life as a *drink-offering,* rejoicing in it.[47]

The pride, the arrogance of his education, the hate and his flesh were crucified on the Cross of Jesus, purified and refined as gold in the fire of the Holy Spirit, with the only purpose that his beloved Jesus could make His abode with him and become one with Him in sacrificial love: "I have been crucified with Christ; it is no longer I who live, but Christ who lives in me; and the life I now live in the flesh I live by faith in the Son of God, who loved me and gave himself for me," (Galatians 2:20). The apostle Paul learned to love God and his neighbor because the sacrifice of Jesus on the Cross was part of his life. He learned that the Lord loves all his children, and finds them worthy of His unconditional love and of the ultimate and selfless sacrifice, the death of His Son Jesus on the Cross.

The Lord wants to redeem humanity, to save them from eternal damnation. Jesus opened the doors of heaven for His children to live with Him eternally. If God loves each one of us like this, why not to love ourselves and our neighbor as he or she is? The apostle Paul wrote that God is our "maker, we are His masterpiece, for we are what he has made us, created in Christ Jesus for good works, which God prepared beforehand to be our way of life," (Ephesians 2:10).[48] Realize dear reader, as the apostle Paul did, how much love God the Father and His Son Jesus Christ have for you. Then, material things lose all their luster, and greed, vanity, and lust, appear to you as they really are, deceptions; they take away your attention from the only reality that matters, God's immense love for you.

When we experience the love of God, with the help of the Holy Spirit, separation from sin is not a hurdle, but a radical response to the radical love God has for us. God broke the chains that kept us shackle to sin, and we feel truly free, really grateful to God, for our freedom, with an exuberant, lasting happiness that comes from a grateful heart. Christians, who have made radical changes in their lives to let God dwell in them, enjoy God's love, so real and present that they will pray at all times to keep sin far, for not losing their friendship with God.

Awareness and meditation on the life of Jesus, what He did for us on the cross, and on His love for us has the mighty power of God to transform our lives. This can only be achieved through His Holy Spirit dwelling in us. If we dedicate time to our loved ones, to know all we can about them, with more reason we need to dedicate time to God to know Him better, by studying and reflecting in His Word. We need to pray at all times, and look for the Lord early in the morning and at night in the secret of our rooms to have a conversation with Him. We talk to God as we will talk with a loved one, to whom we trust. Like in any conversation, we need to have periods of silence that let us hear what the Lord wants to tell us through His Word, through His Holy Spirit, trusting that God always hears us: "The LORD is near to all who call upon him, to all who call upon him in truth," (Psalm 145:18).

When we are really experiencing the love of God as Paul the apostle did, the world may deny the existence of God, yet, we know by experience that He is with us, because He is real to us. God is the very source of our joy and peace, even if there is suffering in our lives. His love for us is not an emotion or a feeling, but we know by experience, that Jesus is with us every day of our lives. Whatever the circumstances, Jesus is always available to hear us at any time: "When you search for me, you will find me; if you seek me with all your heart," (Jeremiah 29:13). In times of sorrow, we experience God's peace and consolation. We know we are not alone in our sufferings, but

Jesus is always with us and for us. Thus, Paul wrote to the Corinthians:

"Blessed be the God and Father of our Lord Jesus Christ, the Father of mercies and the God of all consolation, who consoles us in all our affliction, so that we may be able to console those who are in any affliction with the consolation with which we ourselves are consoled by God,"(2 Corinthians 1:3-4).

Jesus Christ, the Son of God, by coming to this world in human form, was able to share and to experience with us, His beloved children, our daily lives, our sufferings and joys, our material and spiritual poverty:

"And being found in human form he humbled himself and became obedient unto death, even death on a cross. Therefore, God has highly exalted him and bestowed on him the name which is above every name, that at the name of Jesus every knee should bow, in heaven and on earth and under the earth, and every tongue confess that Jesus Christ is Lord, to the glory of God the Father," (Philippians 2:8-11).

Paul the apostle experienced the unconditional love of God, as a certainty, as a conviction, that could carry him through every circumstance. The situations of danger, and the changing circumstances, between having material things, food, and not having anything at all, did not bother Paul, because he learned to depend on God's love and in His providence. Paul said that He was never in need because God is all he ever needed; God's strength carried Him through all:

"Not that I was ever in need, for I have learned how to be content with whatever I have. I know how to live on almost nothing or with everything. I have learned the secret of living in every situation, whether it is with a full stomach or empty, with plenty or little. For I can do everything through Jesus Christ, who gives me strength," (Philippians 4:11-13).[49]

God gives direction to our lives; He teaches us the right path to follow through His Word. We partner with Jesus in this adventure, because the goal is to live eternally with Him. The Word of God is His ancient wisdom, so many times tested by humankind, and all who followed it by loving God first, and their neighbor as themselves, got the approval of God and His blessings. His word is inspired by the Holy Spirit[50] to teach us to live right with Him, with ourselves, and with others. Thus, when asked which commandment in the law was the greatest, Jesus responded:

"'You shall love the Lord your God with all your heart, and with all your soul, and with all your mind.' This is the greatest and first commandment. And a second is like it: 'You shall love your neighbor as yourself.' On these two commandments hang all the law and the prophets," (Mathew 22:37-40).

If we love God and our neighbor as ourselves, we are at peace. Only Jesus was able to teach us about the Kingdom of God because His Kingdom is about *righteousness, peace, and joy in the Holy Spirit*;[51] this is the secret of happiness! When we don't do anything that causes our neighbor harm, or suffering, we don't suffer, or at least we stop any struggle that could cause suffering to ourselves and to others. As a result of God's love for us, our actions become more loving, kind, peaceful, and compassionate.

CHAPTER 4

GOD'S FAITHFUL LOVE

"But you, O Lord, are a God of compassion and mercy, slow to get angry and filled with unfailing love and faithfulness."
—Psalm 86:15—

God's Word is our anchor to the truth. God does not change; His Word is always the same: "God is not a human being, that he should lie, or a mortal, that he should change his mind. Has he promised, and will he not do it? Has he spoken, and will he not fulfill it?"[52]

Societies, (the Bible calls them the world or the fallen world), are in constant change; they go in different directions with ideologies, customs, and philosophies, according to politics, culture and traditions, making anyone confused, even causing many to wander and find themselves lost. The solution to this problem is the powerful knowledge of God and His Word, to discern what is true and good, and to learn how to live with the dignity and righteousness of being children of God:

"Every Scripture is God-breathed (given by His inspiration) and profitable for instruction, for reproof and conviction of sin, for correction of error and discipline in obedience, [and] for training in righteousness (in holy living, in conformity to God's will in thought, purpose, and action), So that the man of God may be complete and

35

proficient, well fitted and thoroughly equipped for every good work, (2 Timothy 3:16-17).[53]

Paul in his letter to the Colossians warns us:

"As you, therefore, have received Christ Jesus the Lord, continue to live your lives in him, rooted and built up in him and established in the faith, just as you were taught, abounding in thanksgiving. See to it that no one takes you captive through philosophy and empty deceit, according to human tradition, according to the elemental spirits of the universe, and not according to Christ. For in him the whole fullness of deity dwells bodily, and you have come to fullness in him, who is the head of every ruler and authority," (Colossians 2:6-10).

Once we are anchored in God's knowledge, and enjoy a relationship with God the Father through His Son Jesus Christ, we do not want to sin or go back to a life of sin, according to the flesh; we don't want to return to that life we had before the Lord's grace called us to a new life in Him. John the apostle says that *sin is lawlessness*, (1 John 3:4); sin is the voluntary transgression of the Law of God. [54]

When we violate His commandments, we become children of disobedience,[55] doing contrary to the love and the will of God for us. Sin is an error, a willing fault, a mistake that does not let us develop our full potential as human beings. Sin offends the Holiness of God and the love of neighbor, and it is disobedience and rebellion that separate us from God, unless we sincerely repent, and live a holy life through His Grace. Sin is missing the mark[56] to the calling of the Lord to live a holy life, which is the optimal state of the soul to live an abundant life.

God's love does not change, He will always be there for us, but we must take a decision whether we want to live right with God or not: *Don't you realize that you become the slave of whatever you choose to obey? You can be a slave to sin, which leads to death, or you can choose to obey God, which leads to righteous living,* (Romans 6:16).[57]

The Lord gave us His Holy Spirit, to help us live a spiritual life of freedom from sin, of righteousness, of great peace and contentment. If we want to experience the fullness, and the very best of the Christian life, we must live separated from sin with the help of His Holy Spirit dwelling in us. We should have in mind the price Jesus paid to set us free from the slavery of sin and not to abuse the Grace of God sinning by complacency. Yet, if we sin, we can always pray to God, through His Son Jesus Christ and ask Him to forgive our sins:

"My little children, I am writing this to you so that you may not sin; but if anyone does sin, we have an advocate with the Father, Jesus Christ the righteous; and he is the expiation for our sins, and not for ours only but also for the sins of the whole world. And by this we may be sure that we know him, if we keep his commandments," (1 John 2:1-3).

Despite our sins, Jesus loves us and touches us with His Grace to repentance, and cleanses us from all our sins with His precious blood if we ask Him. Jesus loves each one of us with preferential love, tenderness and great compassion. He loves us whether we love Him or not, whether we care for Him or not, because God's love for us does not depend on our feelings, sensations, or actions; but His love is always present, absolute and immutable. God's essence is love; thus, His love for us is faithful, regardless of the actions of humankind. [58] His love is unconditional: *But God shows his love for us in that while we were yet sinners, Christ died for us,* (Romans 5:8).

God's love is immeasurable, and has no end: *Love never gives up, never loses faith, is always hopeful, and endures through every circumstance. Prophecy and speaking in unknown languages and special knowledge will become useless. But love will last forever!* (1 Corinthians 13:7-8).[59]

God's love is faithful, perfect, flowing constantly, merciful, unconditional, and the very source of life. He is the spring of our happiness and peace. His love is present in all His creation. The beauty and splendor of all God's creation show the Glory of the Lord, a testament to His children, the Maker's seal of authenticity, and a living memorial of His immeasurable love.[60]

Jesus never rejects anyone who comes to Him with a willing heart to know Him. Throughout Jesus' ministry, we see Jesus teaching with all patience and love because knowledge of God is His mighty power to transform our lives. His Word is true knowledge that breaks through our darkness and ignorance; the Light is eternal and gives birth to life, (John 1:10). Jesus is *the true light, which enlightens everyone,* (John 1:9). God's light uncovers our darkness and transforms it into light, illuminating all our inner being. Jesus said: *I have come as a Light into the world, so that whoever believes in Me [whoever cleaves to and trusts in and relies on Me] may not continue to live in darkness,* (John 12:46).[61]

God's love is faithful and caring, from the very second we are conceived, till the moment we die to this life, and enter into eternal life with Him. There is no death for Christians, but after this earthly life, we will live eternally with God the Father and His Son Jesus Christ, who is *the radiance of God's Glory and the exact representation of His being,* (Hebrews 1:3).

Jesus said, "I am the resurrection and the life; he who believes in me, though he die, yet shall he live, and whoever lives and believes in me shall never die," (John 11:25-26). This is our faith, our hope, and our conviction: The Lord will transform us into His image and likeness, overcoming the darkness in us, and will raise us by the power of His resurrection to live with him, as children of the family of God forever and ever! [62]As children of God, this is our confidence, that He meets all our spiritual and material needs, *according to His riches in Glory,* (Philippians 4:19).

God gives to His children not necessarily what they ask, but what His children really need. He gives them what it is best for them, to train them, to perfect them, and make them apt citizens of the Kingdom of Heaven, for they will reign with Jesus and with the Father forever, (2 Timothy 2:12).

His Holy Spirit dwelling in us is a manifestation of His faithful love, comforting and teaching us, *revealing to us the deep things of God,* (1 Corinthians 2:10). God knew because He loves us, that we needed a Christian community. We cannot live alone our most Holy Christianity; it must be lived, experienced and shared with others. If Christianity is not shared, there is no spiritual growth, and we cannot receive the fruit and the gifts of the Holy Spirit.

The Lord gives us His Holy Spirit to comfort us and to help each other in our Christian communities, through the gifts of *prophecy, a word of knowledge, healing, speaking in languages and their interpretation.* [63] The fruit of the Holy Spirit dwelling in us is His *love, joy, peace, patience, kindness, generosity, faithfulness, gentleness, and self-control.*[64] We need a fruitful spiritual life for a rich relationship with God and a successful Christian life.

We need the Church, our Christian community where the love of God is shared with our brothers and sisters in Christ. We go to Church to listen to the Word of God, and through His Holy Spirit, we are inspired and the Word of God counsels us. We encourage one another in our faith by studying together the Word of God. We sing hymns and songs to praise the Lord and worship together. We pray for the needs of one another, and do missionary work, reaching people with the Gospel. At the center of our Spiritual life is the faithful love of God, through His Son Jesus Christ, He is with us, His children, and fully part of the family of God, sharing and praying with us in His house that is our house too.

God the Father gave us His only Son, even when He knew beforehand, the suffering and the kind of death the Son was going to endure to save us. This is radical, true love beyond our comprehension! So much the Father loves humanity, so much the Father desires that we learn to live a happy life here on earth, and eternally with Him, that He gave us *His only begotten Son,*[65] to live among us, and quench the thirst of our souls for

God. The Son made known the heart of the Father to humanity: *No one has ever seen God. It is God the only Son, who is close to the Father's heart, who has made him known,* (John 1:18). Jesus, the Son of God, came down to earth, taking a body to be near to us because He loves us.

Think deeply in the Gospel, dear reader, and realize the immense love God has shown for you by giving His only Son, Jesus, to redeem you by dying on the cross. Then, and only then, you will be able to love Him without ever having the need to see Him. God has a love for you that goes beyond human reasoning and beyond your intellect.

When you are touched by the mighty grace of God, while reading His precious Words in the Bible, you will realize His unconditional love for you, the joy of his salvation will invade you, and you will rejoice. If you have begun your journey with Jesus and have started to experience the joy of His salvation, you will find that your joy will increase when you discover and better comprehend His word, by reading the Bible every day. You will discover how great His love is for you, for humankind, and for all of His creation. Paul wrote to the Ephesians from a prison in Rome about growing spiritually in the love of Jesus and getting to know Him better:

"I pray that from his glorious, unlimited resources he will empower you with inner strength through his Spirit. Then Christ will make his home in your hearts as you trust in him. Your roots will grow down into God's love and keep you strong," (Ephesians 3:16).[66]

God's love for us is so great and infinite that is beyond our understanding. We need to meditate on His love and become really conscious of his living love for us and in us. His love is more than a feeling; it is the certainty that His love is real and faithful; even more, it is a conviction! It is faith in God! It is the trust of a child in his Father, knowing that he is loved, and there is nothing to worry about; hence, the child sleeps placidly and peacefully in the loving arms of his Father, with absolute abandonment!

Paul writes to the Ephesians and to us, about trust in God, the faith that grows as we know Him better, through the Word of God: *And may you have the power to understand, as all God's people should, how wide, how long, how high, and how deep his love is. May you experience the love of Christ, though it is too great to understand fully. Then you will be made complete with all the fullness of life and power that comes from God*, (Ephesians 3:16-19).[67]

God is reaching to each one of us through Jesus, to our reality, to show us love. There is no condemnation, no judgment for the one who listens to His Word and practices it, (Romans 8:1; John 12:47); but His tender, compassionate, and faithful love is always reaching for the ailing, suffering humankind, under the burden and the curse of sin, to forgive us and get us right with Him! In fact, for His infinite love for us, Jesus came down from Heaven, to be the cure for the illness and addiction to sin, to meet with each one of us in our brokenness, in our corrupt and sinful reality, to transform it and restore us to health:

"He heals the brokenhearted, and binds up their wounds," (Psalm 147:3); "He himself bore our sins in his body on the tree, that we might die to sin and live to righteousness. By his wounds you have been healed," (1 Peter 2:24).

Thanks for the Father's mercy and compassion for us! Through His Son Jesus Christ, we are able to feel God as One with us, feeling Jesus Christ, so close and personal, talking to us through His Word, walking with us in our daily life, and accompanying us through His Holy Spirit: *Without having seen him you love him; though you do not now see him you believe in him and rejoice with unutterable and exalted joy. As the outcome of your faith, you obtain the salvation of your souls,* (1 Peter 1:8-9).

Indeed, we rejoice in the fathomless love of God, because the Son of God descended from heaven to reach for us. Jesus loves each one of us with preferential love and walks with us through our joys and sufferings! Now, we have an open line to talk to God, whenever we need Him, for the rest of our lives, through prayer:

"And this is the confidence which we have in Him, that if we ask anything according to His Will He hears us. And if we know that He hears us in whatever we ask, we know that we have obtained the requests made of Him," (1 John 5:14-15).

Who else can understand us as Jesus does? For we have suffered many disappointments in our years living in this fallen world. Jesus suffered thirst, poverty, and was rejected by His own people.[68] Jesus' friends, relatives and even the people of His own town, Nazareth, where Jesus grew up, did not believe

Him, and doubted Him; they disregard His numerous miracles that pointed to our Lord Jesus Christ as the Son of God and their awaited Messiah.[69]

Jesus suffered disappointments; many of those, whom he healed, failed to even thank Him.[70] Jesus was hated and persecuted by His own people, who plotted how to murder Him.[71] Jesus was deserted by His closest friends, relatives, and even felt His Heavenly Father had abandoned Him, when He needed the Father the most.[72] When Jesus most needed of His friends, they abandoned Him and betrayed Him.

Judas, one of Jesus' apostles betrayed Him with a kiss, Peter denied Him, while the other apostles ran away.[73] Jesus *felt sorrowful and troubled even to death*, (Mark 14:34). Jesus, at the prospect of the physical punishment and losing His life, prayed in his anguish even *more earnestly, and his sweat became like great drops of blood falling down to the ground*, (Luke 22:44).[74]

Jesus was mocked, insulted, spit upon, beaten, slapped and slandered.[75] Jesus suffered horrifying torture, and even in His innocence, endured a death reserved for the worst criminals; He was sentenced to die on the cross.[76] So faithful is the love of the Son of God, that even in excruciating pain and in agony, Jesus Christ prayed for us, and provided for His mother, leaving her to the care of his beloved apostle John, who was present at His crucifixion and accompanied His beloved mother during those very sorrowful moments.[77] Even in his death by crucifixion, Jesus is the poorest of the poor, naked, possessing nothing. In life, Jesus *did not have a place even to lay his head;*[78] in His death, Jesus did not have a tomb. Thanks to God's providence, to the intercession and generosity of Joseph of Arimatea, a secret follower of Jesus, it was possible to rescue Jesus' body to give Him a proper burial in a new tomb; Nicodemus, a Pharisee and a member of the Jewish ruling council, provided the expensive spices to embalm Jesus for His burial.[79] Even before his birth, Jesus experienced great persecution and poverty. Jesus' hardships since infancy, such as being born in poverty in Bethlehem, and his family's migration to the desert of Egypt due to persecution and then to Nazareth, [80] are common to billions of people in all continents who live in poverty,[81] and to refugees and immigrants around the world who leave their countries because of religious or political persecution, wars, lack of opportunities, famines and poverty.[82]

Even in the most extreme circumstances, thousands of people around the globe can identify with Jesus because they also have suffered torture; millions of people have been displaced and have lived in occupied countries; millions of people have been murdered for their political and religious beliefs. Christians, since the beginning of Christianity, to present times, have suffered persecution, torture, decapitation and crucifixion in most continents and nations, simply for being followers of Jesus.[83]

Jesus Christ's popularity that has transcended the ages is due to His selfless sacrifice on the Cross to save humankind, and His solidarity and compassion for the suffering humanity. He is not strange to our sufferings, and material poverty. For many of us Christians, Jesus is a family member; He is one of us, who lived lacking commodities, but He was rich in love.

This shows the faithfulness of God to all! Jesus was indeed during His life on earth, one of us!

We also can identify with Jesus' many ordinary experiences because this is what we experience in our daily lives. Like many of us, Jesus' had a trade; he was a carpenter and lived with His family. He was living like any other human being until the time was at hand to accomplish His mission. Jesus Christ's life was so common to all before His ministry, that when Jesus started to teach in the synagogue, hearing His Wisdom and seeing His miracles,[84] the people of His town asked: *Is not this the carpenter, the son of Mary, the brother of James, and Joseph, and of Judas, and Simon? And are not his sisters here with us? And they were offended at him,* (Mark 6:3). Paul's letter to the Hebrews, says that Jesus has "sympathy."[85] The word "Sympathy," means to suffer with the other, to understand and care for the feelings of the other:[86] *Since he himself has gone through suffering and testing, he is able to help us when we are being tested.* (Hebrews 2:18).[87]

Jesus Christ has true compassion for us; He is moved by our feelings, and shares them, because of the suffering He endured. Jesus Christ had a great deal of suffering during his ministry and His crucifixion. It was emotional and physical pain, surpassing the measure of pain any one of us could experience in ten lifetimes. We need to feel confident of Jesus' faithful love, compassion and solidarity in every circumstance of our lives. Jesus shares in our joy, but also our sufferings; Jesus is with us in every situation, especially when we endure hardship and sorrow:

"For we have not a high priest who is unable to sympathize with our weaknesses, but one who in every respect has been tempted as we are, yet without sin. Let us then, with confidence draw near to the throne of grace, that we may receive mercy and find His grace to help in time of need," (Hebrews 4:15-16).

The word "compassion,"[88] is used frequently throughout the Bible: *The LORD is good to all, and his compassion is over all that he has made,* (Psalm 145:9). The Merriam-Webster Dictionary defines compassion as, "the *sympathetic consciousness of others' distress together with a desire to alleviate it.*"[89] Indeed, this is what God the Father, and His Son Jesus Christ feel for us. God has compassion for our sufferings, and hardships. It is Jesus' desire to alleviate our suffering. For this reason, God sent His Son Jesus Christ, to *seek and save the lost,* (Luke 19:10); Jesus is the faithful love of God for humanity. We are never alone in our sufferings:

"Blessed be the God and Father of our Lord Jesus Christ, the Father of sympathy (pity and mercy) and the God [*Who is the Source*] of every comfort (consolation and encouragement), Who comforts (consoles and encourages) us in every trouble (calamity and affliction), so that we may also be able to comfort (console and encourage) those who are in any kind of trouble or distress, with the comfort (consolation and encouragement) with which we ourselves are comforted (consoled and encouraged) by God,"(2 Corinthians 1:3-4).[90]

God's compassion and faithful love for humanity brought Jesus to earth to be our light in our darkness. Jesus said: "I have come as light into the world, that whoever believes in me may not remain in darkness," (John 12:46); darkness is the denial of life itself. Jesus Christ came for us *to have life, and have it more abundantly*, (John 10:10). Jesus is God, and One with the Father, but for our sake, He *was made flesh* [91] to teach us how to live right with God and our neighbor. If we practice His Word, we live in His glorious light, in His knowledge, and we stop living in darkness. God's Word in the Bible is the true knowledge we need to reach our real potential as human beings, to live right with God, and as citizens in our societies and more importantly, in His heavenly Kingdom.

If we live according to the truth that Jesus reveals to us in His Word, we receive His peace, hope, and contentment. These gifts do not depend on the material things we have or the difficulties we bear in life, but in the certainty that God's love is faithful: *He who did not withhold his own Son, but gave him up for all of us, will he not with him also give us everything else?* (Rom 8:32).

When the Spirit of God is living in His children, they bring the Kingdom of Heaven to the world, by practicing love of neighbor. By imitating Jesus' loving actions, we learn how to truly *love God and our neighbors as ourselves*, (Mark 12:30-31). The Father, through His Son Jesus Christ, sent to us His Holy Spirit, to help us, to encourage us, to teach us the Gospel, the good news to all people, (John 14:25). Jesus is a *fountain of living water* that does not grow dry; Indeed, *it is a spring of water gushing up to eternal life*, (Jeremiah 2:13; John 4:14).

The living Word of God changes our hearts and transforms us into His likeness. Its seed multiplies in the hearts and in the

48

minds, when we preach the Gospel as Jesus commanded us, making the world better, one person at a time: *And he said to them, Go into all the world and proclaim the good news to the whole creation.* (Mark 16:15). Christians are *the salt of the earth, but if salt has lost its taste, how shall its saltiness be restored? It is no longer good for anything except to be thrown out and trodden under foot by men,* (Matthew 5:13). The salt gives flavor and enhances the aroma of our food; salt is the oldest method to preserve food. On the same token, Christians who abide in the love of God, perform actions that give a lasting flavor of love to the world, preserve our most Holy Christianity, and enhance the aroma of a fragrant and pleasing sacrifice to God!

Jesus said: *I am with you always, to the close of the age,* (Matthew 28:20). God's faithful love is always with us and dwelling in us. God never gives up on us, unless we decide that we don't want Him in our lives. Who can despise true love and our very happiness? As difficult as it is to conceive, there are those who reject our Lord Jesus Christ, and the saving love that he offers to all.

The most important decision we will ever make is to give our lives to Jesus and to follow Him. Jesus went willingly to the Cross, to atone for our sins and to reconcile us with the Father:

"For if while we were enemies, we were reconciled to God through the death of his Son, much more surely, having been reconciled, will we be saved by his life. But more than that, we even boast in God through our Lord Jesus Christ, through whom we have now received reconciliation," (Romans 5:11).

Jesus made a way to heaven for us, His children, to give us eternal life with Him: Truly, truly, I say to you, he who hears my word and believes him who sent me, has eternal life; he does not come into judgment, but has passed from death to life, (John 5:24).

As we experience the caring and infinite love of Jesus Christ, we cannot help, but to touch each person we meet with the love of God. By extending our hands, our hearts and our faith to all, we spread His love and His word to the entire world. The joy of His amazing love abiding in us Christians cannot be contained, and needs to be shared with others.

The eternal flame of Jesus' love dwelling in us and His Holy Spirit, compel us to give ourselves in service to God, by serving others. Let's share the Grace that touched our hearts with God's amazing gift, our Salvation!

—THE END—

BIBLIOGRAPHY

[1] Bible references are taken primarily from the New Revised Standard Version Bible. In less measure, we take Bible references from the *Holy Bible*, New Living Translation, (NLT), and "The Amplified Bible Classic Edition, (AMPC)" These last two Bible versions are annotated in the bibliography. The Bible verses in italics are for emphasis.

[2] Philippians 4:7.

[3] NLT

[4] NLT

[5] 1 John 5:14-15, Romans 4:25

[6] 2 Corinthians 4:4.

[7] Ertelt, Steven. Expert Told Congress Unborn Babies Can Feel Pain Starting at 8 Weeks. May 12, 2015. On Line: http://www.lifenews.com/2015/05/12/expert-told-congress-unborn-babies-can-feel-pain-starting-at-8-weeks/ . Last consulted: June 1, 2016.

[8] Chambers, " 21st Century Dictionary." Hopetoun Crescent, Edinburgh. Chambers Harrap Publishers, Ltd. 1999. Pg 484.

[9] NLT

[10] AMPC

[11] NLT

[12] AMPC

[13] AMPC

[14] Matthew 7:14.

[15] John 7:38.

[16] Revelation 4:6.

[17] Zephaniah 3:17.

[18] Joshua 1:8; Psalm 119:97; Psalm 1:2; Genesis 24: 63; Psalm 63:6; Ps 77:3,6,12; Psalm 119:15,23,27,48.78.148; Psalm 143:5; Psalm 145:5; Luke 21:14. " הגה. (haĝaĥ): To moan, growl, utter, muse, mutter, meditate, devise, plot, speak, to roar, growl, groan, to utter, speak, to meditate, devise, muse, imagine, to utter, to mutter." The Brown-Driver-Briggs Hebrew and English Lexicon. Oxford, Clerendon Press, 1906. Public Dominion.

[19] Isaiah 12:3.

[20] NLT

[21] Luke 17:21

[22] NLT

[23] Philippians 3:20.

[24] John 14:2.

[25] 2 Corinthians 11:16-28.

[26] 2 Corinthians 12: 7-8.

[27] Acts 22: 4-5.

[28] Gigot, F. (1909). Gamaliel. In "The Catholic Encyclopedia." New York: Robert Appleton Company.Retrieved August 24, 2016 from New Advent on Line: http://www.newadvent.org/cathen/06374b.htm. Last consulted: August 24, 2016.

[29] Acts 22:3.

[30] Ibid.

[31] See Acts 6-7.

[32] Mark 8:18.

[33] Acts 9:4-5.

[34] Acts 9: 7-8.

[35] Sulpitius Severus. *Sulpici Severi Chronica*. Liber Secundus, 29. Of the death of Paul by decapitation, and Peter by crucifixion. The Latin Library. On Line: http://www.thelatinlibrary.com/sulpiciusseveruschron2.html. Last consulted: May 30, 2016. See also Quintus Septimus Florens, Tertullian. "Prescription against Heretics." Chapter XXXVI. "The Apostolic Churches the Voice of the Apostles. Let the Heretics Examine Their Apostolic Claims, in Each Case, Indisputable. The Church of Rome Doubly Apostolic; Its Early Eminence and Excellence. Heresy, as Perverting the Truth, is Connected Therewith." Christian Classics Ethereal Library. On Line: http://www.ccel.org/ccel/schaff/anf03.v.iii.xxxvi.html. Last Consulted: May 30, 2016.

[36] 1 Peter 2:5.

[37] NLT

[38] 2 Corinthians 5:17.

[39] NLT

[40] Romans 12:18.

[41] 1 John 2:9.

[42] Proverbs 19:11.

[43] NLT

[44] NLT

45 2 Corinthians 12:9.

46 Ephesians 2:9-10.

47 Philippians 2:17.

48 NLT

49 NLT

50 2 Timothy 3:16.

51 Romans 14:17.

52 Numbers 23:19.

53 AMPC

54 1 John 3:4; John 13:35; 1 John 4:12.

55 Ephesians 2:2; 5:6.

56 Sin: ἁμαρτία (hamartia), "to err, to miss the mark." Thayer, Joseph, H. "Greek-English Lexicon of the New Testament." New York, NY. U.S. Corrected Edition. American Book Company.

57 NLT

58 1 Corinthians 1:9.

59 NLT

60 1 John 4:18; Malachi 3:6; Hebrews 13:8; Job 12:7-10.

61 AMPC

62 1 Corinthians 6:14.

63 1 Corinthians 12:7-11.

64 Galatians 5:22-23

65 John 3:16.

66 NLT

67 NLT

68 John 19:28 2 Corinthians 8:9: Philippians 2:7;Mark 6:1-6; Mark 6:4.

69 John 12:37-40; Mark 6:1-6; Luke 4:16-30.

70 Luke 17:14-18.

71 John 15:18-25; Luke 22: 2; Matthew 12:14; Mark 14:1; Matthew 26: 2.

72 Mark 14:50; John 16:32; Matthew 26:31; Matthew 27:46.

73 Matthew 26: 33-34; Mark 14:30; Mark 14:72; Mathew 26: 56,75;

74 Matthew 26:37-38; Mark 14:33-34; Luke 22:44.

75 Matthew 26:67

76 Luke 22:63-64; John 18;22; Matthew 26:67; Mark 14:65; Matthew 27:33-50; Mark 15:25-32; Luke 23:32-42.

77 Luke 23:34; John 19:25-27.

78 Luke 9:58.

[79] Matthew 27:57-60; John 19:38-42; Luke 23:50-53; Mark 15:42-46; John 3:1-20; John 7:50-51.

[80] Matthew 2:1-23.

[81] World Bank on Poverty. On line: http://www.worldbank.org/en/about. Last consulted: May 12, 2016.

[82] Migration Policy Institute. On line: http://www.migrationpolicy.org/programs/data-hub/maps-immigrants-and-emigrants-around-world. Last consulted: May 12, 2016.

[83] Breitbar: Report: ISIS Has Crucified, Tortured Thousands of Christians in Iraq, Syria: http://www.breitbart.com/national-security/2015/09/29/report-isis-crucified-tortured-thousands-christians-iraq-syria/. Last Consulted: May 12, 2016. Reuters: Islamic State committed genocide against Christians, Shi'ites: U.S. On line: http://www.reuters.com/article/us-mideast-crisis-usa-genocide-idUSKCN0WJ1OL. Last consulted: May 12, 2016.

[84] Mark 6:2-3.

[85] sumpatheo͞, (συμπαθέω). Thayer, Joseph, H. "Greek-English Lexicon of the New Testament." New York, NY. U.S. Corrected Edition. American Book Company. Harper & Brothers, 1989.

[86] Sympathy: "the feeling that you care about and are sorry about someone else's trouble, grief, misfortune, etc. : a sympathetic feeling. Merriam Webster Dictionary.

[87] The King James Bible 1611 translation of the word "sympathy," (sumpatheo͞), is "touched with the feeling of our infirmities," (Hebrews 4:15).

[88] From the Hebrew רחם(raḥam): compassion, mercy. The Brown-Driver-Briggs Hebrew and English Lexicon. Oxford, Clerendon Press, 1906. Public Dominion.

[89] Merriam-Webster Dictionary. On Line: http://www.merriam-webster.com/dictionary/compassion. Last consulted: May 12, 2016.

[90] AMPC

[91] John 1:14.

ABOUT THE AUTHOR

Beatriz Schiava felt called by God to share the love of God through her books. She has more than 40 years studying the Word of God and frequently shares the love of God with Christians and no Christians alike. Beatriz studied a master in theology at Notre Dame University, and also has a master in international affairs from Washington University St. Louis. Beatriz is a retired medical doctor, who enjoys spending her time helping others to understand the Bible and taking care of her family. Beatriz congregates in a nondenominational Church in St. Louis Missouri.

SOCIAL MEDIA

Beatriz shares posters, and commentaries on the Bible through social media. Find Beatriz' new books on her web page, social media, or Amazon.com.

Beatriz' website page:
www.ancientchristianitypress.com

On twitter:
@ChristianInst
https://twitter.com/ChristianInst

Facebook:
https://www.facebook.com/AncientChristianity

Pinterest:
https://www.pinterest.com/christianinst/

NOTES

www.ingramcontent.com/pod-product-compliance
Lightning Source LLC
Chambersburg PA
CBHW070457050426
42449CB00012B/3013